GOLF

Do the 2 go together?

Introduction

Is it okay to say God and Golf in the same sentence?

Having played professional golf for over four decades, I have often wondered if God is ever with me on the golf course. How about you? What do you think? Well, I can most assuredly tell you that he is! Although, as Billy Graham once said, "It seems the only place God doesn't answer my prayers is on the golf course."

Just who or what is making that ball always curve towards the nearest lake, pond or sand trap? Why is it, if trees are 90% air, the ball always hits that one lone branch? Why when I tell myself "Don't hit it left towards the Out of Bounds," that is exactly what I do? How is it that on some days I can play like Jack Nicklaus or Tiger Woods, and on other days it seems like I have never picked up a club?

Is God for me or against me?

Let me tell you my fellow golfer, God is there on the course and I think He is often getting a good laugh at our inability to control that little white man-made object (or whatever color ball you play). On some days the golf ball seems to have eyes, knowing exactly where the bottom of the cup is, and yet on other days it seems to be allergic to the little round hole, always moving away from the cup at the last moment (or not going near it at all).

But isn't that what we love about this game? The unknown? Oh, I'm not talking about the new course you've always wanted to play when I say the "unknown." I'm talking about not knowing how we are going to play that day. Will it be Woods like, or "woods like?" Will we play like Jack or will we play like a hack? On those days when it's Jack or Woods like, we are in the best of moods. On most of the other days when it's hack in the woods like, we are depressed, that is, until we can get out there and play again.

What is it about this game that keeps us coming back for more punishment, usually week in and week out? I have written this little prose as one of the Pros who has loved and hated this game for over 40 years. And like you, either way I can't wait to get out there and play it again.

I want you to know that God and Golf can be in the same sentence, depending on how you use these two terms. Some people use God's name on the golf course quite a bit. Unfortunately, it is often followed by two other words (d.... it), making "God" out to be the problem when in reality it was our in-ability to hit the shot required or the shot we wanted.

Yes, golf is a four-lettered word. But I've heard less cussing by a proverbial group of sailors than I have in some rounds of golf. If golfers happen not to take God's name in vain, then usually I hear them use this one; "Jesus Christ," and I assure you they are not praying. How come people don't say "Aww Buddha, or "Blasted

Muhammed"? Why is it always God and Jesus?

Either way, golf is both frustrating and exhilarating. It is humbling and satisfying. That's why we keep playing this stupid game, right?

Let me take you on a short "golf outing."

Pastor Gary

Chapter One

IN THE BEGINNING

I was introduced to golf when I was 15 years old. I'm over 55 now, so you do the math. I was blessed to have some great golf teachers, guys like Bob Martin, Bob Kessler and Johnny McMullen. Each of them took me under their wing and taught me the finer points of the game and the swing.

I was a baseball player originally. That was my first love. And like many of you, I was going to make it to the Big Leagues! That is until a career ending injury happened to me at age 15.

I was raised in Oakland California where I grew up playing baseball in the inner city with the likes of Ricky Henderson and Dave Stewart, and a number of other players who went on to the Big Leagues.

I was usually the only white guy on "all black" teams. I made it to the Oakland All-Stars five years in a row. I was a pitcher and 3rd baseman/shortstop and I was really good. I threw a 3 hit shutout at the age of 9 to win the city championship and always batted lead-off because of my speed and hand-eye coordination. My high school coach, Mike Margoulis, had waited 3 years for me to come to Oakland High School to play for him.

The summer I was going into high school, our team, Porter House, in Oakland, made it to the quarter finals of the city championship. Because I had not lost a game pitching in over 3 years, my coach gave me the assignment to pitch the quarter final game. We won, and the next day was to be the semifinal game.

My coach had a huge ego and he came up to me and said, "You are pitching again tomorrow." It was (and I believe still is) illegal to pitch a kid more than 7 innings in one week. Because I was afraid of him, I acquiesced and said yes. My arm was a bit tender from pitching all 7 innings of the quarter final game, but the next day there I was again.

As I was warming up before the game, I could tell my arm was sore. But being only 15, I was afraid to say anything. As the game went on, my arm was getting increasingly sorer. Finally, in the 6th inning I told one of the other players on my team how sore my arm was and he said I should tell the coach. My fear of him (he weighed about 220 lbs.) caused me to not say anything.

The last play of the game was a ground ball back to me on the mound, and I literally threw the ball in the dirt to first base; my arm was gone. Little did I know that I had torn everything in my shoulder and my baseball career was over.

However, we won that game too, and two days later was the City Championship game. But, I had to play first base because I could not throw at all. By the way, we lost!

As High school started (we started high school at tenth grade back then), the coach Mr. Margoulis asked me to come to the baseball try outs. I couldn't throw at all. My arm was gone and the pain was simply too much. Baseball was over! Or so I thought.

My friend Mike Johnson saw how depressed I was and asked me if I wanted to go play golf. I said, "Golf? That's a sissy game." He eventually talked me into it and I was surprised at how fun it was. I signed up for the golf team, and that first year we were horrible. So was I. But because I was an athlete, I began to practice really hard. My junior year I had the lead going into the last round of the High School City championship but threw it away on the 15th hole at Lake Chabot golf course.

My senior year, I was determined to win the High School City Championship, again to be held at Lake Chabot golf course. I shot 71-71 in the first two rounds and had a 4 shot lead. But I ballooned to a 77 in the last round and got in a playoff with the best putter in our district. If you have ever played Chabot, the first hole may be the most challenging on the course. Up over a rise, down a valley and then uphill to the green. Chabot was always known for its excellent greens and he and I both had 4 foot putts for a chance to win.

His ball was outside mine by about 2 inches, so he went first. He missed! Now the tournament was mine to win or lose. Those four footers are nothing when goofing off with buddies, but when it means something… Well, you know. But somehow I made it. I won the High School City Championship in only my 3rd year at golf! I was hooked!

Chapter Two

CHASING THE DREAM

I was raised in a Christian home by two godly parents who took us to church multiple times a week. My brother Dave and I, knew the Bible better than most kids our age, but it had little effect on us in our early years. Or so I thought. By age 16, I told my mom I wasn't going to church anymore just because she wanted me to go. I said I would go when I wanted to, which by the way, was almost never. Big mistake.

Now, I know some of you had a bad experience with church growing up. Whether it was Catholic or Protestant, or another denomination, you saw way too much hypocrisy in the so-called "believers." So did I.

Except for my parents, that is. They were genuinely godly people. Oh they had their faults, but they really loved the Lord. Their routine, EVERY MORNING, was to be in the living room praying and reading their Bibles. I witnessed this my whole young life. We constantly had beautiful Christian music playing in the house, and looking back, it was an awesome experience.

By age 18, I had begun to drift far away from my Christian roots. Like many young people today, I wanted to experience life outside the church walls. I began partying and having fun. I started to drink on a semi-regular basis, but what I really enjoyed was the cannabis. We didn't call it that back then. You know what we called it.

I had more girlfriends than I should have, but life was fun, at least that is what it looked like. But often times I would go home at night and just feel like something was missing. I would shrug off the tension that came from partying like everyone else or living the life I had learned from my parents growing up, thinking they were old fashioned and too "holy" for me. Golf and girls-that was it for me. And the partying!

At age 19, I had quit college, was working for a painting company, and lived in my own rented apartment so I could really party. I was going nowhere fast. Every Sunday morning a bunch of us guys would go up to Merritt College and play tackle football, no pads. I would, more often than not, play quarterback. It was crazy playing tackle football with no pads with guys who weighed well over 200 lbs.

I am 5'9" and have always weighed about 170 lbs.

One Sunday after the game, I went home and realized if I could throw a football 45-50 yards, I could throw a baseball again. The next day I moved out of my apartment, moved back in with my parents and signed up at DVC College in Pleasant Hill, California, so I could go back to my first love, baseball. I signed up for the baseball team and after a couple of months of trying out, I was cut from the team for the first time in my life. It was a very humbling experience.

But I wouldn't let that stop my childhood dream, so I went down to Laney College in Oakland and signed up for the baseball team there.

I played well at Laney and also joined a semi-pro team in El Cerrito. My skills were coming back quickly after being out of the game for four years, and I eventually ended up at Chabot College playing under Coach Don Christianson.

While I was playing for the El Cerrito Braves one day at Bushrod Park in North Oakland, I had an exceptional game, going 4 for 4 at the plate and throwing out 7 guys from shortstop. At the end of the game, an older black gentleman approached me and the first baseman, Joe Silva, and said he was a Los Angeles Dodger's scout. After watching us both play that summer, he said we were invited to come play winter ball for the Dodgers.

We both did back flips in excitement and couldn't wait for our opportunity. Unfortunately, the Dodgers moved their camp down to southern California, but another scout who had his eye on us invited us to the San Francisco Giants rookie camp. This was a dream come true. As a kid I would listen to the Giants on radio for hours. Willie Mays was my hero.

I played for a while with the Giants organization but felt the coach wasn't giving me a fair chance.

Because I was a hothead and a loner, I quit the team. Probably one of the dumbest moves of my life. I made myself believe golf was my sport, but baseball had always been my first love. I began playing golf halfway seriously but wasn't improving much. I was just chasing girls and partying and playing golf because I didn't want to do much else.

By the time I was 21 years old, I had begun to take the game a little more seriously and thought about making it a career. I started to change my practice habits.

Instead of getting up at 10:00-11:00 am each morning after partying most of the night, I began getting up at 7am and practicing most of the day. The pay-off was worth it.

I was becoming one of the top amateurs in the Bay Area, finishing in the top 10 in most of the amateur events.

But something was about to drastically change my life.

Chapter Three

A massive change in my life

At the age of 22, I was dating an older woman, playing golf and partying. That was my life. In addition, I was a die-hard Raiders fan.

But something was missing in my life. One day I was playing the old Alameda south course and on the first hole, and as I was walking down the fairway, I prayed under my breath and said, **"Lord, would you really help me if I turned my life towards you?"**

I had about 110-yard wedge shot into the green for my second shot and after praying this prayer, I hit the wedge and the ball flew right into the cup! I am not joking. Talk about God getting your attention…

A couple of weeks later on Monday night, November 17, 1980, I was sitting in my buddie's apartment in Alameda watching the Raiders play the Seattle Seahawks on Monday night football. We were partying as we usually did, when all of a sudden,

I realized that my life was going nowhere. Here I was, dating an older woman (which, by the when she was younger, had been a Christian), partying most nights of the week, playing amateur golf (where you do not get paid), with no real direction or vision in my life.

About halftime that night, I stood up and said, "I gotta go." "Go where?" my friends asked. "Go to church," I said. "CHURCH? Man, the Raiders are playing," they said. So I got up and drove my 67' mustang to a little church in north Oakland that my dad attended and sat in the back row. Looking back, it took a lot of guts to get off that couch and leave my buddies, knowing they would ridicule and tease me. But I had to do what was right and best for me.

As I sat in the back row of that church, a young black evangelist was preaching. He began to talk about how much God loves us and how he sent His son to die on the cross to pay for ALL OF OUR SINS.

No matter what you have done, he said, if you will confess your sin, God will forgive them all. "All?" I thought. Even the stuff I had done that I wasn't proud of? He said that God loves every human being so much that He gave up His only son,

Jesus, to die on the cross for the sins of the whole world.

As I listened to him talk about God having a distinct plan for every person and how much He truly wants to bless us with joy and peace and favor, I could feel my heart shifting inside me. Even though I was sitting there with my arms folded thinking, "You're not getting to me, preacher," I couldn't help but feel like he was talking right to me. I was empty inside. Even though on the outside I may have looked like I had a pretty cool life, there was something missing. Something that sex or partying or friends just couldn't fulfill. Have you ever felt that way? Empty?

At the end of his sermon he had what they call an "altar call." Basically, that is when after the preacher is done preaching, he asks if anyone wants to accept Jesus Christ as their Lord and Savior. As I sat there fighting off the thoughts and feelings that it was time to make a massive change in my life, the preacher said, "Are you ready to accept the love of God in your life?"

For what seemed like an eternity (it was really only 20-30 seconds), I fought with my thoughts.

"Are you ready to do this?" I thought to myself. "What about girls? What about weed? What will your buddies say? What if you are no good as a Christian and you fail God?"

All these thoughts, I realized, were from the devil trying to keep me - from accepting God's love. I began to remember the things I had been taught as a little boy that "Jesus came to save sinners." I sure fit into that category. I remembered that Jesus didn't come to call people who think they are righteous or good, but for people who would acknowledge their sinfulness and ask for God's forgiveness. All of a sudden I found myself getting out of my seat and walking down the aisle towards the front of the church. I was the first one to move towards the front, but then another and another began to come forward. I distinctly remember having this thought, "Jesus, if you could die for me, then I can live for you." I started crying. Then I started sobbing. All I can tell you is the love of God enveloped me and I gave my life to Jesus Christ right then.

That was November 17, 1980.

CHAPTER FOUR

God, I thought you were there for me?

Back in the late 70's and early 80's, the California State Amateur Championship was held at Pebble Beach and Cypress Point Golf Courses! Did you get that? Cypress Point, one of the most prestigious Golf Clubs in the country, if not the world. Every good amateur wanted to qualify for that tournament, not just for the chance to win, but to play those courses. I was blessed to have played three years in a row.

The tournament format was two rounds and then a cut, and then a third round and another cut down to the low 64 players. This one year, I bogeyed the last hole to get in an 8-way playoff for 7 spots. That means only one guy wasn't going to make it. Being a brand new Christian, I was a shoe-in, right?

I mean, God is for me and loves to bless His children. But there are other lessons in golf that He likes to teach us besides just winning.

As we stood on the first tee at Pebble Beach to start the playoff, I sensed the Lord tell me in my heart, "I'm here with you right now." I started smiling on the first tee, even though no one knew why. "I got this," I thought to myself. I had not missed one fairway all day at Pebble Beach, not one; 14 for 14.

When my turn came to tee off, I stood up on the first hole and proceeded to hook the ball right over the fence into someone's backyard! Out of Bounds. Guess who got eliminated? Yep. Me. The Christian kid. I couldn't believe what I had just done. Needless to say, I was confused about this God stuff.

As I began to drive home, thoroughly depressed and more than a little upset with God, I stopped and picked up some comfort food at a fast food drive thru. I put my drink on the dashboard, looked in the bag of food, and then drove off with the drink still on the dash. Instantly the whole thing spilled on my lap, staining my plaid colored pants.

It was at that moment I realized the devil wanted me mad at God for not giving me what I wanted. I became acutely aware that God was teaching me a very valuable lesson that I would need thousands of times in my life; **"Can you still praise me when things don't go your way?"** came that still small voice inside of me. You see, when I got eliminated from the playoff, I didn't feel like talking to God for letting me down (like He was the one who hit the ball out of bounds).

If we really think God is the one directing our golf ball when we play, then how can we boast or brag when we make a hole in one, or a double eagle, or a 30-foot putt? There may be moments when God "allows" our ball to hit a tree and go out of bounds, or hit that one rock sticking out of the pond and the ball ends up in the middle of the fairway, but more than likely, God uses these "breaks" to teach us character and self-control.

Shouldn't we be thankful every time we get to play golf? Good days and bad, golf is a privilege and a blessing to be able to play. The beauty of the outdoors - a mountain lake on the finishing hole or an environmental area which man can't touch - the setting of each golf course is unique and beautiful, some more than others.

I remember one day when I was out playing, it felt like army golf, you know, off to the left then off to the right. Left, right, left… I was grumbling and complaining about my swing, my clubs, the guys I was playing with, anything and everything. Then I looked over and here was a guy playing golf with only one arm. One arm! I said, "Lord, I'll try never to complain again. Thank you for letting me play this wonderful game."

WHEN THINGS GO YOUR WAY

How do you feel when on those rare days, everything goes your way? Isn't that the best feeling ever? Well, at least one of the best. I say that because the very next day it can go the complete opposite. I had one of those great days before, just like you have. Let me tell you about it.

It was 1983 and I was attempting to qualify for the United States Amateur Championship to be held in Glenview Illinois that year. There are multiple sites to choose from when it comes to National Championships so I chose Peach Tree Country Club in Marysville, California because I had played some events there before.

It is an older tree-lined course with doglegs and small greens. A good challenging test. I wasn't playing exceptionally well before this event so my hopes of making it weren't too high. There were only four qualifying spots out of 50 players trying and many were among the top college players around. This was a 36-hole qualifier with all 36 holes played in one day.

I bogeyed the first hole but made a 20 footer on the 2nd hole Par 5. I just kept plugging along and found myself 2 over par going to the 18th hole par 5 and somehow managed to make a birdie for an opening round 73! Not bad for not having my "A" game.

The temperature was 105 degrees outside and they didn't have any food prepared for us. So, after a short break you immediately teed off again for the 2nd round. I hadn't eaten anything.

I had two different caddies that day and also a few friends following me around. I was even par going to my 16th hole of the second round (I started on the back nine in the second round), a long par 3 over water. I hit a 2 iron right at the pin and it came to rest just off the back edge of the green about 18 feet from the cup. It was a short "touchy" chip, downhill on fast greens. I had worked real hard all summer on my short game and it was about to pay off.

I hit this slippery chip and it trickled down and fell right into the cup for a birdie 2. That placed me at 1 under for the round and even par for the day. There were two holes yet to play but I still didn't think I was going to make it. My caddie, who is now an attorney in Oakland, Ivan Gold, came up and said to me, "I still think you need one more birdie." What are friends for?

I hit my drive on this par 4 down the middle and my approach shot ended up 36 feet away for birdie. It was slightly uphill with a little break to the left. My coach, Bob Martin had always said, "Always try to hit a perfect putt, and if it goes in, great." So I tried to hit a 36-foot putt. About 6 feet from the hole, I could tell it had a chance, and to my amazement, it fell right in the center of the cup!

Now I was 2 under on the round and 1 under for the day.

The 9th hole (my 18th in the 2nd round) is a short dogleg left par 4 with a small green. The pin was tucked left and the green dropped sharply away if you missed it left on the short side. I will admit I was nervous standing over that short iron and I came right over the top of the shot and missed the green left. I could feel the blood run right out of my veins. I knew I had just blown my chance to play in the U.S. Amateur.

When I got to my ball and assessed the situation, it would require a flop-type-shot and I would have to stop it fairly quickly. As I said, I had been working on my short game all summer long and was pretty good around the greens, but this shot, under the circumstances, would require all my finesse. My coach Bob Martin had always told me to work on your short game four hours for every hour you hit golf balls.

I hit the shot and it came to rest just 4 feet past the cup. Not bad from where I was. But now I had to wait about 5 minutes before I could attempt this final putt. The other 2 guys I was playing with seemed to take forever to line up and hit their putts and I was getting more nervous by the second.

You know all those voices you hear when you have an important shot to make: "Don't pull it." "Should I hit it firm and straight or soft and play a little break?" "Is it inside the cup or just off the edge?" "What if I miss?"

"Am I going to throw it all away on this one putt?" Those demon voices just wouldn't shut up!

But then I remembered a verse in the Bible, 2 Timothy 1:7, "God did not give us a spirit of fear; but of power and love and of a sound mind." I began quoting this verse over and over, "God did not give me a spirit of fear. God did not give me a spirit of fear."

After lining up the putt, I determined it was just inside right edge. I reminded myself I had made a 4 footer to win the high school championship and told myself I could do it again. I went through my routine which I had been using all day, stood over the putt and rolled it right in the heart of the cup!

All my friends, both my caddies and my girlfriend, starting cheering and clapping when I made the putt. Now, there was only person standing in my way, Robert Meyers from Brigham Young University. He was a top player and very well known. The USGA official was on his radio talking with another official to see if there was anyone else close enough to qualify still on the course.

I heard them talking and one of them said, "Robert Meyers is the only guy left on the course with a chance. He is even par for the day and is on 9th hole right now" (his 18th hole in the second round). I saw his tee shot land right in the middle of the fairway, so just I couldn't bear to watch. I went behind the clubhouse with my girlfriend and just prayed.

Robert hit his approach to 15 feet and I knew he was going to make his birdie putt to tie me. That's all I needed, a playoff with one of the best college players in the nation. I waited for what seemed like forever, and when I came around the building the official was standing there and said to me, "You made it, you're in, Robert missed the putt!"

I have to admit, that was one of the coolest feelings to receive my certificate to play in the 1983 United States Amateur. I honestly couldn't sleep that night.

CHAPTER 5

God had other plans for my life

I turned Pro shortly after the U.S. Amateur. I didn't want to play for "store credit" anymore. I wanted to play for real money. So I declared myself a professional and began chasing the mini-tours around the western United States. My friends said I should still play amateur golf for the experience but I was determined to play with the "Big Boys."

My first tournament was in La Jolla down in So-Cal, a 3-day event. I finished 9 shots behind the winner, but as I was driving home, I was going over the round and realized I had 3 putted 9 times! I thought to myself, "If I eliminated the 3 putts, I could have won my first pro event.

I drove home with great determination to fix this problem and get ready for my next event in Walnut Creek, at Boundary Oaks golf course. This was to be a 2-day event. This is a strong and challenging course. It is not a super long course, but the greens can be fast and treacherous. If you are above the hole and the greens are fast, it's almost a guaranteed 3-putt. This would be a good test to see if I had fixed my putting problems.

I shot 72-72 and tied for 1st place!

Now I would be in my first playoff as a professional. How would I handle the pressure? We both made par on the first hole and the second hole is a downhill par 3, about 165 yards. I played first and hit it to about 15 feet from the hole. He hit his shot, and believe it or not, his ball landed right on my ball on the fly! What are the odds of that? His ball careened about 30 feet away and my ball was to be placed back where it was when he hit it.

My opponent 3 putted from 30 feet and I won with a 2 putt. I was victorious in only my second professional event. I went on to win 5 tournaments and placed high in a few others.

Later that year I went to play in the Queen Mary Open down in Los Angeles where 238 pros teed off in that tournament. Guys like Loren Roberts, Bob Tway, Steve Pate and Ernie Gonzales. This was a stacked field.

I opened with a 69 in the first round and followed that up with a 72. Good enough to make the cut into the weekend. The third round was one of the most solid rounds of golf I played that year. I only shot 70, but I played smart and never was in any trouble. I didn't make a bunch of putts otherwise it would have been even a lower round.

In the fourth round I continued to play solid golf and after shooting 35 on the front nine, proceeded to birdie holes 10 and 11. I must have gotten nervous because I three putted a couple holes late in the round but hit a wedge to 6 inches on hole number

18, and finished with a 68! Good enough to finish tied for 7th. Not bad out of 238 players.

Now it was time to try to qualify for the PGA tour. This would be four rounds at the Butte Creek Country Club in Chico, California. But God had other plans.

When I got saved in 1980, four years earlier, I really fell in love with the Lord Jesus. I was the number one player at Chabot College for two years and I carried a black golf bag the first couple of months before we got our team bags. I took a paint brush and with white paint I wrote, "Jesus Loves Me" in large letters on my bag. People didn't know what to make of me. My coach, Jay Yarborough, knew I was serious about God and wouldn't let the others make fun of me. I didn't care. I was so full of joy from being a born-again child of God.

I began teaching a Bible study on Monday nights in the home of some friends of mine, starting with just six people. But it just kept growing and growing. We had as many as 35 people in their tiny living room coming to hear the Word of God.

They would sit on the couch, in chairs, and all over the floor. People were getting healed, saved, and delivered from all kinds of addictions and habits of life. I knew God wanted me to be in the ministry, but I wanted to play professional golf.

At the PGA tour qualifier in Chico, I hit the first 27 fairways and was still 2 over par. Then I missed the 28th and 29th fairways going double bogey, double bogey. Needless to say, I wasn't going to make it. It was during the fourth round that I realized God had other plans for me.

Some of you might be saying, "You gave up to soon." But before you do, let me tell you what happened.

During the 4th round, everyone in my foursome was out of the running to qualify for the tour. But these guys were still taking up to 5 minutes to hit a putt! As I was standing on the 3rd green waiting my turn, it dawned on me, "This is a waste of my time. Touching people with the gospel of Jesus Christ is what I'm supposed to be doing." At that moment, the dream of being a professional golfer just died. It died inside me. That's the only way I can describe it.

I literally quit in my heart. Oh I still loved golf, but as for making it a career, God wanted me for other things. That may not be for everyone, but it was for me. It was at that moment that I knew what my life's calling was.

Within a couple of years, I would be the pastor of my first church!

CHAPTER 6

What does golf mean to you?

What is your favorite golf course to play? Mine is Olympic Club, The Lake course. That is one of the most demanding courses around. I believe it was Ben Hogan who said, "Olympic Club is a ball striker's golf course." It has more hills than most people realize and because it is right on the ocean at sea level, it plays even longer, especially with the cold air and fog.

If you could play any course before you die, which one would you want to play? Pebble? Saint Andrews? Augusta? (Good luck with that one). Mine would be Augusta National. But I think only God could get me on there. Whatever course it is, just be thankful that we live in a country where we still have our freedoms and we get the PRIVILEGE to play this great game.

That's why there is no need to get so upset at yourself when you play; you are just not that good. LOL. I'm teasing. But why not be competitive with a good attitude instead of a bad one?

My brother has a picture hanging in his office of some golf course somewhere, and at the bottom it says, "To play good golf, one must be calm with a cool attitude". If you are anything like me, you are competitive and you hate to lose. When we mess up or blow a shot, the tendency is get upset, say things we shouldn't and sometimes act a fool. But that's because we forget it is a privilege to just be out there.

Most likely you are not going for the tour, but even if you are, think about Fuzzy or Trevino, and the attitudes they displayed on the course. Tom Watson was another cool customer. Put a smile on your face and realize that golf is full of double bogeys and bad shots. Sometimes we choke and more times than not, we are simply not quite good enough. But you can still thank God for the enjoyment of this game.

Presidents play it, bankers, plumbers, chefs, housewives and gentlemen of all kinds. The way our country is headed I don't know how much longer we will have these freedoms, so enjoy it while you can. And, the Bible says in the book of Revelation that one day "all the GREEN

GRASS will be burned up!" Yikes. Better get a round in this week before it's too late.

We have a bunch of guys from our church who play every Thursday morning. We play anywhere from Poppy Ridge in Livermore to Alameda golf course, and all points in between. Occasionally we take a trip to Yoche De He up at Cache Creek or down to Monterey and play Del Monte or Bayonet. When one of the guys turns 50, we have even played Pebble Beach. It is great fellowship of a group of guys who love Jesus and have a good time together. So what about you?

What has golf done for you? Has it molded your character at all? Are you learning self-control? Integrity? Honesty?

I'm in my late 50's now, and in 2017 at age 58, I signed up to try and qualify for the U.S. Open. Again, there are multiple sites to choose from so this year I chose Yoche De He, at Cache Creek. A beautiful and challenging course with fast greens.

Now, mind you, I was 58, playing against all those young college bucks. That day I hit 16 greens and two par 5's in two. Unfortunately I three putted both of them and hit a ball in the water on hole 16. With those three shots thrown away, I still fired an even par 72 and missed by one shot, again! I say again because I have missed 8-10 times by one shot. I know, God is trying to tell me something.

Twice in the U.S. Senior Open I missed by a shot. One of those times I was in a 6 way playoff for the second spot (they only have 2) and lipped out a nine footer to get in, only to lose the on the 3rd playoff hole.

The other time was my first attempt at this championship and I missed a 4 footer on the last hole and finished 3rd. OH well, that's golf.

GOLFERS CAN'T COUNT

It is amazing to me that guys can't count when they play golf. In tournaments you have to keep another guy's score, so I'm trained to always keep track of my "opponent's" score. But some guys just forget or don't know how to count. Don't let that be you. Golf is about integrity you know.

Maybe there are things God wants you to learn through the game of golf. Things like, it's usually best when you hit the ball down the middle of the fairway (translation; take only paths in life that are sure). If you keep getting off the straight and narrow in life, sooner or later you will end up in a hazard, in the woods, or committing an unforced error.

But like golf, there simply is no way to be "bogey free" in life. By that I mean, you are going to sin and do stupid stuff in your short life. God is a Holy God and sin breaks fellowship with Him. But he loves us so much that He himself provided the payment for our sins, His Son Jesus Christ. When you realize you are a sinful individual and God can't fellowship with sin, and you acknowledge that Jesus paid for all your sin by shedding His blood on the cross, and you then accept Jesus Christ as your Lord and Savior, God removes all your sin from you, all of it. It's like a mulligan at life.

Jesus rose from the dead to prove He is God's son and that He is Lord of all. He wants to give you a new start at life. Yes, He can heal your marriage, mend that relationship with your kids or your parents. He can heal your body and even turn your business around. But all that is secondary to Him loving you and dying on the Cross for you. But it is up to you. Your golf game may or may not improve (you probably need some golf lessons), but your life surely will.

If you were to die without accepting Christ as your Savior, you are NOT going to "make the cut" in God's tournament. Only He "qualifies" you to make it to the "finals" (Heaven). There is no other way. Jesus made this statement; "I AM THE WAY, THE TRUTH, AND THE LIFE. NO MAN COMES TO THE FATHER EXCEPT THROUGH ME."

Jesus proved His Lordship by being raised from the dead. So now you know. What will you do with this new "lesson"? The choice is yours.

I am here if you need me. My email and phone number are in the back of this book. The person who handed this booklet to you can probably help you as well.

Maybe one day we will play together. It would be my pleasure.

EPILOGUE

Here is a simple prayer that if you pray from your heart, can change your world forever.

"God, I come to you now, and I am a sinner. In fact, God, my sins are many. But you said you loved me so much that you sent your son, Jesus, to die on a cross for me. I acknowledge my sin to you and ask you to forgive me. I accept Jesus Christ as my LORD and SAVIOR. I do believe that Jesus rose from the dead and that he is Lord of all. Teach me your ways Father God. Fill me with your Spirit. Put me in a good Bible teaching church where I can grow and learn.

Thank you Father. In Jesus name, Amen."

If you prayed that prayer with a sincere heart, the Bible says you are saved. Romans 10:9 says, "If you believe in your heart that God raised Jesus from the dead, and confess with your mouth, Jesus is Lord, you are saved."

Be blessed my friend,

Pastor Gary

Faith Fellowship Worship Center

577 Manor Blvd

San Leandro, Ca. 94579

pastorgarymortara@yahoo.com

Made in the USA
Columbia, SC
08 November 2024